Legal review of

Surrogacy

Hossein Ghasemi

Title: Legal Review of Surrogacy
Author: Hossein Ghasemi
Publisher: American Academic Research, USA
ISBN: 9781947464179

Author's Speech:

A good book, from the humble point of view, is to express the mind of its author. In other words, it is better for the writing on the paper to be largely in line with the author's theory of thought, so that when one reads the book one receives the same as if one were attending a lecture by the author of the book.

I have tried it too, but I do not know how successful I have been in this direction.

The present work is more research than authorship; But the same amount of his writings is the result of the perception of a law student from the valuable books and theories of the great jurists of Iran, and if you see a mistake in the text, it is the result of my misunderstanding that God willing it will be corrected and completed in the future.

Therefore, if you have a theoretical article in the form or nature of a disagreement with the author or more complete, please send it to the following e-mail address to be reviewed and applied in future editions.

In the end, I consider it necessary to express my gratitude for the efforts of my dear friend, Dr. Hossein Shokrian Amiri, Professor of Jurisprudence and Law of Mazandaran University, who clarified the way for me as a bright light.

Hossein Ghasemi
2022-5-10
H_vakil@yahoo.com

Table of Contents

Introduction

Family and the need to have children are among the emotional and expedient rights that are recognized for each couple according to each society. Fertilization or pregnancy in the course of human history has always been natural and without the intervention of external factors, and based on what was realized until a few decades ago, any couple who were incapable of natural fertility and fertilization were considered infertile, but advances in modern science Medicine and the development of its tools have led to the occurrence of some natural complications that prevent some couples from being able to conceive naturally and go through the process of natural reproduction, in some ways treating themselves and the background To provide for childbearing and pregnancy experience (Behjati Ardakani, 2001).

According to biology, there is a gap of about seven days from the time of fertilization to the beginning of its replacement in the uterus, and this is the beginning of the fetus in the uterus and pregnancy, and if this does not happen, small infertility has occurred.

Of course, regardless of the identification and introduction of infertility syndromes that are different in men and women, in the discussion of artificial insemination, there are different types, which can be called intrauterine and extra uterine fertilization.

Rental uterus or surrogate uterus is a very popular term. In this case, the man and woman have fertility, but the woman has a problem with the structure of her uterus or no uterus at all. Therefore, this woman's egg is adjacent to her husband's sperm, and after the formation of an embryo in another woman's uterus, this embryo is replaced and returns to the arms of its original parents after birth (Akhundi, p 21, 2005).

Uterine rental is one of the methods of artificial insemination or in vitro fertilization, which is the most controversial type of artificial insemination according to the principles of our legal jurisprudence. This debate has very wide dimensions that always make the legal community to be more interested in research and study on understanding the various aspects of this issue and the effects and rulings that are imposed on it.

The uterus of some women is not able to go through pregnancy and carry the couple's fetus for various reasons, but it generally lacks the problem of insemination. In this case, the couple asks another woman to keep the fetus in her womb for nine months of pregnancy during a contract, and in short, this process is called surrogate mother, rented mother, or nursemaid. The subject of a rented mother, as mentioned, has no history of narration in the past of Shiite jurisprudence, but there are bubbles – I mean problems - of this subject about fertilization and pregnancy of a woman who was married and had husband but also she was lesbian, or narrations about adultery and The quality and the reasons for it can be visualized. Given the above, the importance of research on the subject of rented uterus is clear. In this article, we will look for a rented womb in Iranian jurisprudence and law.

Hossein Ghasemi

Chapter One

Generalities and concepts:

Since in any research, generalities should be stated about the subject under discussion, before the main topics, so in this chapter, under the heading of generalities and concepts, we will examine the generalities and concepts related to the subject.

- ## First speech: Concepts

1-1-1-The concept of Surrogacy:

A surrogate mother or surrogate mother is a method in which a woman (surrogate mother) carries the child of a couple who are unable to conceive in the usual way. This method is traditionally performed by first fertilizing the real mother's ovum and the father's sperm by artificial insemination and then replacing the embryo with artificial insemination inside the mother's uterus. In this case, the woman carrying the fetus is only a host to the fetus and has no genetic involvement with the resulting fetus. In such a case, the father's sperm is fertilized in vitro by the mother's ovum, and the fetus is replaced in the womb of another woman who can conceive, and the newborn inherits the genetic characteristics of his parents.

According to Shari'a, the surrogate mother has the status of a foster mother and legally has legal validity (Rouhani, 2014, p. 87).

The agreement of the infertile legal couple to use the womb of another woman to transport the fetus belonging to them and, finally, the delivery and return of the newborn to the couple, is realized mainly in the form of a contract of supplication. The parties to the contract in this contract are, on the one hand, an infertile couple and, on the other hand, the adoptive mother of the fetus ("surrogate mother"), and According to the general rules of contracts, it is the written will of these two parties that leads to the emergence of the legal action in question.

In a surrogacy contract, a woman as a surrogate mother agrees, at the request of a couple, to carry the fetus during pregnancy, in the order prescribed in the contract, to give birth to the fetus as their child and then deliver the baby to them. Leasing of persons is subject to ordinary rules of renting based on the terms of contract and the validity of the contract. That is, it is a reciprocal contract in which the interests of the hired worker and the recipient must be legitimate, rational, definite and possible. The action of the surrogate mother in the surrogacy contract can be thought of in two ways: One is that the surrogate mother, in return for a certain exchange, appropriates a special benefit of herself, the main one of which is reserved for the uterus, to the parents, and commits herself to perform certain basic and necessary tasks such as necessary examinations and tests and care for the fetus. Another is that it can be imagined that the surrogate mother undertakes to conceive for a certain wage by the fetus belonging to the ruling parents and by enduring the pregnancy period and its conditions, the fetus should be kept and nurtured in its womb and after childbirth, the baby should be delivered to them. (Katozian, p. 574). It seems that the use of IVF technology (in vitro fertilization) in uterine replacement has led to different definitions of surrogate uterus. According to some researchers, the concept of motherhood used in surrogacy should be removed from this word because the purpose of surrogacy is not to strengthen the position of motherhood. There are other topics for uterine replacement, including pregnancy replacement, host replacement, IVF replacement, surrogate uterus, or borrowed uterus. Researchers have also used various terms for infertile couples with gametes, including potential parents, formal parents, candidate parents and legal parents (Moeini, 2007, p. 28). Thus, a comprehensive definition of uterine replacement can be providing: Uterine replacement is a method for infertile couples to have a child, according to which a woman with a uterus becomes pregnant from a fetus resulting from the fertilization of sperm and ovum of the infertile couples by assisted reproductive methods and undertakes to deliver the baby to the applicant's infertile couple after pregnancy and childbirth based on the contract concluded between her and the couple's legal couple. The infertile couple is considered to be the real parents and the pregnant woman who carries the pregnancy as a surrogate mother (Hojjat, 1996, p. 59).

1-1-1-1-History of Surrogacy:

The use of a surrogate mother or surrogate mother first occurred in the late twentieth century. This action was the result of the activities of a lawyer named Noel Yakn in the United States. He founded several organizations operating under the Alternative Maternity Act in the United States. The first agreement to pay a surrogate mother was made in 1980 in the United States. Following the agreement, a 37-year-old woman, nicknamed Elizabeth Bacon, agreed to accept to be a surrogate mother for $ 10,000.

Despite the legal and ethical restrictions on the use of these methods, about 6,000 births by uterine replacement were reported until 1997 in which there were only 500 births using advanced methods of in vitro fertilization (IVF) have been in uterine replacement.

Iran also started its medical measures with a ten-year delay in inventing IVF methods in the world. Infertility Treatment Center at Yazd University was established for the first time in 1988 in Iran in cooperation with the ART Center of the University of Germany and after that, various research medical institutes were set up in public and private centers and are still active and providing medical services. (Hamdollahi 2009, p. 15).

The plan to use another woman's uterus was implemented around 2001 by some fertility clinics in Iran. However, various medical, cultural and legal restrictions on the use of in vitro fertilization technology in the use of third parties in the reproductive cycle have slowed the treatment process or stop doing it when the ground is not ready, but this method of treatment makes hope for those who wish to have children. Iran is one of the best equipped countries in terms of infertility treatment and all IVF methods are used to treat infertility in the country. Advances in infertility treatment have made Iran a main country for alternative IVF treatments in the Middle East. The reason is the existence of facilities such as providing facilities in subspecialty centers and government-affiliated centers, Iranians are Shiites and Shiite scholars agreeing to fertility by uterine replacement using in vitro fertilization techniques and cheaper infertility treatment costs in Iran compared to other countries.

1-1-1-2- Types of alternative uterus:

The use of surrogacy technique as a solution in the infertility treatment process has different types and divisions, which are divided into three groups based on the origin of the ovum used to create the fetus.

1-1-1-2-1- Complete replacement:

Complete replacement or replacement in pregnancy is the same as using another woman's uterus and transferring the couple's fetus. In this case, the ovum and sperm of the infertile couple are transformed into embryos by IVF method, and while coordinating an infertile woman requesting a surrogate uterus and a lady possessing a uterus, the resulting fetus is transferred to a surrogate uterus and the lady who has the uterus carries the fetus belonging to the infertile couple in her womb until the time of delivery. In this method, the surrogate mother has no genetic connection with the fetus and the infertile couple are considered as the biological parents of the child (Bagheri Nasab, 2012, p. 30).

1-1-1-2-2- partial replacement:

In relative or partial replacement, another woman's uterus and ovum are used. Because the infertile wife, in addition to not having a uterus or a defect in the uterus, lacks an ovum or a healthy ovum, therefore, a surrogacy mother's pregnancy is the result of in vitro fertilization of the ovum and the sperm of the infertile woman 's husband. The woman who has the uterus is genetically dependent on the child and she is the biological mother of the child genetically and the legal father of the child is also the wife of the infertile woman and the infertile woman has no biological or genetic connection to the child. Some have excluded this type of uterine replacement from the topic of surrogate mother and believe that surrogate mother is the main mother of the child because it is related to the child both biologically and genetically. Therefore, referring to such a woman as a surrogate mother and replacing a surrogate uterus with these explanations is not correct, but the lady with a uterus can be considered as a surrogate mother in another way.

Also, it is true that this woman is the owner of the ovum and uterus, but in fact she has agreed with the infertile couple to use her uterus for the infertile couple and replace her uterus with the uterus of a real mother (Alizadeh, 2006, p. 180).

1-1-1-2-3- Surrogate using donated ovum or embryo:

In this type of surrogate uterus, the infertile couple uses a donated egg or embryo to fertilize the uterus. This operation is divided into two groups due to the genetic relationship of the fetus with the infertile couple seeking the child:

1- Substitute mother using donated egg

This method of uterine replacement is used in cases where the infertile woman not only cannot carry the pregnancy in her womb, but also lacks an egg. Therefore, the sperm of the infertile woman is fertilized with a donated egg in the laboratory and the fetus is transferred to the surrogate mother's uterus. The surrogate mother has no genetic connection with the fetus, but the husband of the infertile woman is considered the legal father of the fetus (Bagheri Nasab, 2012, p. 32).

2- The surrogate mother using the donated fetus

If the man has no sperm and the woman has no egg, or the couple's sperm and egg are not healthy enough to reproduce and the infertile woman's uterus is able to hold the fetus and breed and give birth, then the fetus is ready for both men and women. Who are strangers to each other or taken from legal couples are implanted in the uterus of an infertile woman. The resulting fetus is not genetically related to the couple but is biologically related to the infertile woman.

Another division that can be attributed to a surrogate mother refers to the type of agreement or contract between the surrogate mother and the foster parents, depending on the monetary relationship between the foster parents and the surrogate mother:

1. Commercial Alternative In this case, the surrogate mother, who is usually a stranger introduced by professional intermediaries, is willing to play the role of surrogate mother in exchange for receiving money from the requesting parents.

2- Non-commercial or altruistic replacement: In this case, the surrogate mother (who is usually a close relative or close friend of one of the parents or both of them) without receiving any money other than reasonable compensation for the costs imposed by pregnancy and childbirth and from Out of love and altruism towards the demanding parents, he is willing to play the role of a mother (Aramesh, 2007, p. 176).

1-1-1-3- Use of surrogate uterus (medically):

- Absence of uterus in woman, which may be congenital or acquired.

- The presence of a uterus with an abnormal structure that may be congenital or acquired again.

- Frequent abortions in women who become pregnant but have frequent miscarriages and no specific cause is found for their abortion.

- Repeated failure of artificial fertilization in cases where couples have used artificial fertilization methods such as IVF or ICSI to conceive due to repeated infertility, and despite producing good quality embryos in the laboratory, it has never led to pregnancy.

- Women who have a chronic illness have been barred from becoming pregnant because of the risk of their disease getting worse during pregnancy or because of the possible side effects of their medications on the fetus, For example, patients with advanced heart disease.

- Prevent the transmission of genetic defects (Mohseni, 2015, p. 29).

- Social reasons

A group of women, although neither they nor their husbands have any physical problems, but for reasons such as job motivation, maintaining fitness, desire for comfort and convenience, escaping the hardships of pregnancy and instead of becoming pregnant themselves, they put the responsibility of pregnancy and childbirth on another woman (Naebzadeh, 2001, p. 82).

1-1-1-4- Limitations of infertility treatment by surrogacy:

Alternative uterine infertility treatment as a new phenomenon in medical science will certainly face medical, legal, cultural and social issues, problems and challenges. Familiarity with the problems of using alternative uterine therapy and its medical, cultural, legal and social limitations is important. Some of these restrictions and prohibitions are:

3- Medical restrictions

Assessment of physical and mental health of infertile couple and lady with uterus by specialists in this regard before treatment, during treatment and after treatment requires the allocation of specialized clinics and treatment clinics to organize and manage alternative maternity services.

2- Legal restrictions

Development and progress of alternative infertility treatment as a new method and a new phenomenon in the field of medicine will be followed by various and new legal issues as needed, and in our country, this new method of infertility treatment without a clear legal framework and rules. It has caused suspicions and differences of opinion in various fields such as: fetal abuse, motivation of the parties to the contract, child custody, etc., which can certainly be answered by formulating a clear and comprehensive law.

3- Cultural, social and psychological limitations

Following the formation and use of any new phenomenon and technology, there is a possibility of abuse of that technology in some societies, so at the same time with the use of new methods of infertility treatment using a surrogate uterus, which is the involvement of a third party in the pregnancy process. The use of this technology in non-medical cases has also become common, and the interventions of intermediaries in the selection or introduction of a third party for pregnancy by an infertile woman have led to brokerage markets that have a commercial aspect, which is a kind of abuse, looting and trading. Commerce with human personality and dignity and degrading the status of motherhood and promoting slavery and exploitation of women in society will be considered, which has led some countries such as Austria, Sweden, Germany and Norway to use the law of no alternative uterus. And many infertile couples have no choice but to go to neighboring countries for treatment. (Behjati Ardakani et al., 2007, p. 23).

1-1-2- The concept of lineage:

Genealogy (lineage) literally means infinity, origin, race, kinship, and interest and relationship between two objects or human beings. Although the first chapter of the eighth book of Iranian civil law is devoted to the rules related to lineage, but there is no explicit definition of the nature of lineage in this law, so jurists have provided different definitions to identify the legal nature of lineage.

To achieve a comprehensive definition of the legal nature of lineage, it is necessary to first examine the definitions provided by jurists and solicitors.

Sahib Jawaher writes in the definition of lineage: "lineage is the end of personal birth to another such as father and son or the end of the birth of two people with a third party, such as two brothers and father" (Najafi, 1409, vol. 11, p. 67). The problem that appears in the above definition is that the connection of birth is in fact the source of validity of the relative relationship, but the truth of lineage is something that is abstracted from the connection of birth, so in this definition there is confusion between credit and the source of credit.

Dr. Emami has defined descent as follows: " lineage is the gerund and means kinship". Then he adds: "lineage is something that is created by the coagulation of sperm from the cohabit of men and women. From this, there is a natural blood relationship between the child and the couple, one of whom is the father and the other is the mother. "(Emami, 1999, p. 174)

Mohammad Boroujerdi Abdeh also writes: "lineage is an interest between two people that occurs due to the birth of one of them from the other or their birth from a third person." Boroujerdi, 2014, p. 56)

The problem that can be seen in these and other definitions related to lineage is that they have defined lineage as a result of the coagulation of the sperm of man and woman and the developmental and real relationship, and since vague words should be avoided in the definition, therefore the above definitions do not seem comprehensive. It seems that the reason for the inconsistency of the concept of lineage in various definitions is due to the way they are defined, that is, some jurists, instead of defining lineage, have defined relative kinship, the scope of which is wider than lineage, and have not defined lineage, in other words, relative kinship and lineage are different.

However, in order to clarify the issue, it is necessary to distinguish a particular lineage from a relative or general lineage and to define each one separately.

General lineage: General lineage or relative kinship is the interest and blood and legal relationship between two people, which is the result of the birth of one of them from the other or the birth of both from a third party.

Among the contemporaries who have discussed this issue is Sheikh Abdul Basit. He says: "If a woman's egg is inseminated with the sperm of a foreign man and the woman is unmarried, the child is attributed to that woman like an illegitimate child and is not attributed to the owner of the sperm, because his sperm is wasted. But if a woman is married, the child is attributed to the man, according to the Prophet (pbuh), who said: "The child is attributed to her wife." Also, if the man is sure that the child does not belong to him, he can deny the child by commination and the marriage is terminated between the two, in which case the lineage of the child is eliminated from the couple and only joins his mother. But if he knows that the child is not from him, but is satisfied with him, the lineage of the child to the husband will be proved, but the husband is a sinner, and if that child is a son, it is obligatory on the daughters of this man to cover themselves from him and observe their hijab, and if the child is a girl, it is a precaution for the sons of this man not to marry him. "(Klini, 1407 hijri, p. 194)

The conclusion is that according to Sunni jurists, the birth lineage of artificial insemination joins the pregnant couple, even if it is from sperm of a stranger. But if the woman is an unmarried bearer, the child does not have a father and only belongs to the mother, contrary to the opinion of Imami jurists who in any case link the child's lineage to the owner of the sperm.

1-1-3- The concept of insemination:

Fertilization literally means pregnancy and female fertility and insemination means female fertilization (Dehkhoda, 1347, 6082).

Others have interpreted insemination as the process of sexual production in which male and female gametes combine to form an egg cell, and has been used in the following sense:

- Introducing the substance of the male palm tree to the female date palm tree to be fertilized.

- Injecting a small amount of vaccine into the body to build immunity

- Inoculation and vaccination

- Transfer of male animal sperm to female and generally fertilization.

It should be noted that whenever this word is used without any restrictions, it means to get pregnant.

1-1-4- The concept of artificial insemination:

Artificial insemination involves a variety of methods in which all the semen or sperm, after being prepared or nurtured, is placed in different parts of the female genitalia and allows sperm and oocytes to collide without sexual intimacy. Therefore, artificial insemination can be considered as the insertion of sperm into the uterus of a woman by medical devices or any other objective device other than sexual intercourse. (Taghizadeh, 2013, p. 67)

In legal terms, artificial insemination is the fertilization or conception of an animal or human and even plants by artificial means (Alavi Qazvini, 1374, 166) Pregnancy of a female animal without natural mating is called artificial insemination. For this purpose, sperm is taken from the male animal and transferred to a part of the reproductive system of the female animal (end of vagina, cervix or uterus) with an inoculation gun.

In medical terms, insemination also means that sperm and egg are combined by medical device or any other means except intercourse and sexual intimacy. Artificial insemination with the husband's sperm and spermatozoon is called homologous insemination (AIH) and with stranger sperm is called heterologous artificial insemination (AID). (Taghizadeh, 4, 2011)

1-1-5- Definition of infertility and infertility:

Infertility and Sterility are called "inability to conceive". If after one year of the couple being together and having a sufficient number of active sexual intimacy and without the use of contraceptives, pregnancy does not occur. According to the latest statistics of the World Health Organization, there are about sixty to eighty million infertile couples all around the world and about more than one and a half million people in Iran. The overall prevalence of this Phenomenon is about ten to fifteen percent, but absolute infertility is estimated at about eight percent. (Sohrabvand, 2005, 7)

Infertility of the ovum (the failure to conceive) is called female infertility and infertility is generally used for women whose problem is primarily "not getting pregnant" Obviously, a woman infertility may be due to defects in her own body or that of her husband, which prevents her from becoming pregnant.

Therefore, the term infertility refers to men and women who have defects and inadequacies that partially prevent them from having children, but these defects are not to the extent that make it impossible for them to have children, and perhaps such couples can have children again automatically or through medical treatment and possibly marriage. Fertility power is defined as the ability to reproduce and requires the necessary ability to start and maintain a pregnancy.

Infertility is the failure to conceive, with no contraception, after one year of regular intercourse in women, means a decrease in the ability to conceive and reproduce.

In general, a woman not getting pregnant after two years of marriage and cohabitation can be considered as a sign of infertility. Of course, in some cases, a period of two years is not necessary for infertility to be applied and a person can find out about her infertility from other signs and evidence. (Soleimani and Azizi, 2017)

1-1-6- Types of infertility:

Infertility can be divided into three categories: primary, secondary, and relative.

1-1-6-1- Primary infertility:

Infertility in which a woman has not seen any signs of pregnancy before, in other words, she has never had a pregnancy before.

1-1-6-2- Secondary infertility:

Men and women who are infertile but have previously married another man and woman and had children in that marriage. In other words, there has been at least one pregnancy before the current problem.

1-1-6-3- Relative infertility:

It occurs in men and women whose genital insufficiency is minor and they have children for a long time, especially if each of them marries another couple who is completely healthy (Soleimani and Azizi, 2001) Thus, infertility is sometimes primary and sometimes secondary. Primary infertility refers to a case in which a couple has never been pregnant, and secondary infertility refers to the fact that at least one pregnancy has occurred in the past and they are now infertile for reasons such as the use of contraceptives. Factors contributing to infertility include genital infections, aging and passing the period of fertility, alcohol and drug injuries, chemotherapy and radiotherapy, as well as chemical toxins and environmental factors.

1-2 Second speech: generalities and principles of generation production:

The problem that can be seen in these and other definitions related to lineage is that they have defined lineage as a result of the coagulation of the sperm of man and woman and the developmental and real relationship, and since vague words should be avoided in the definition, therefore the above definitions do not seem comprehensive. It seems that the reason for the inconsistency of the concept of lineage in various definitions is due to the way they are defined, that is, some jurists, instead of defining lineage, have defined relative kinship, the scope of which is wider than lineage, and have not defined lineage, in other words, relative kinship and lineage are different.

However, in order to clarify the issue, it is necessary to distinguish a particular lineage from a relative or general lineage and to define each one

General lineage: General lineage or relative kinship is the interest and blood and legal relationship between two people, which is the result of the birth of one of them from the other or the birth of both from a third party.

Among the contemporaries who have discussed this issue is Sheikh Abdul Basit. He says: "If a woman's egg is inseminated with the sperm of a foreign man and the woman is unmarried, the child is attributed to that woman like an illegitimate child and is not attributed to the owner of the sperm, because his sperm is wasted. But if a woman is married, the child is attributed to the man, according to the Prophet (pbuh), who said: "The child is attributed to her wife." Also, if the man is sure that the child does not belong to him, he can deny the child by commination and the marriage is terminated between the two, in which case the lineage of the child is eliminated from the couple and only joins his mother. But if he knows that the child is not from him, but is satisfied with him, the lineage of the child to the husband will be proved, but the husband is a sinner, and if that child is a son, it is obligatory on the daughters of this man to cover themselves from him and observe their hijab, and if the child is a girl, it is a precaution for the sons of this man not to marry him.

The conclusion is that according to Sunni jurists, the birth lineage of artificial insemination joins the pregnant couple, even if it is from sperm of a stranger. But if the woman is an unmarried bearer, the child does not have a father and only belongs to the mother, contrary to the opinion of Imami jurists who in any case link the child's lineage to the owner of the sperm.

Fertilization literally means pregnancy and female fertility and insemination means female fertilization (Dehkhoda, 1347, 6082). Others have interpreted insemination as the process of sexual production in which male and female gametes combine to form an egg cell, and has been used in the following sense:

- Introducing the substance of the male palm tree to the female date palm tree to be fertilized.

- Injecting a small amount of vaccine into the body to build immunity

- Inoculation and vaccination

- Transfer of male animal sperm to female and generally fertilization.

It should be noted that whenever this word is used without any restrictions, it means to get pregnant.

Artificial insemination involves a variety of methods in which all the semen or sperm, after being prepared or nurtured, is placed in different parts of the female genitalia and allows sperm and oocytes to collide without sexual intimacy. Therefore, artificial insemination can be considered as the insertion of sperm into the uterus of a woman by medical devices or any other objective device other than sexual intercourse. (Taghizadeh, 2011, p. 67)

In legal terms, artificial insemination is the fertilization or conception of an animal or human and even plants by artificial means (Alavi Qazvini, 1374, 166) Pregnancy of a female animal without natural mating is called artificial insemination. For this purpose, sperm is taken from the male animal and transferred to a part of the reproductive system of the female animal (end of vagina, cervix or uterus) with an inoculation gun.

In medical terms, insemination also means that sperm and egg are combined by medical device or any other means except intercourse and sexual intimacy. Artificial insemination with the husband's sperm and spermatozoon is called homologous insemination (AIH) and with stranger sperm is called heterologous artificial insemination. (Taghizadeh, 4, 2011)

1-2-1- Infertility syndromes:

Another right that can be recounted for a child born in a rented womb is the right to be a legatee, and this right can apparently also be considered for a fetus resulting from IVF. Because the only condition of the will is the presence of the legatee at the time of the will, and this is while the existence of the fetus is that its sperm was coagulated at that time whether this coagulation is in the laboratory or in the uterus. The question now is whether the will is valid for frozen embryos in the laboratory or not? In response, it should be stated that the application of Article 850 of the Civil Code requires that the legatee must be present and be able to own what has been bequeathed to him. On the other hand, Article 851 states that "a will is valid for the fetus, but its possession is conditional on its being born alive." Therefore, being born alive can be considered as a criterion of possession. It should be noted that the law does not even consider abortion as a criterion for the decline of possession because it considers the fetus eligible to have rights. Therefore, Article 852 states: "If the fetus is aborted as a result of a crime, the legatee has the right to inherit it, unless the crime prevents inheritance." On the other hand, some jurists apply the principle of non-existence of this embryo formed in the laboratory environment, because in vitro fertilization and freezing cause the destruction of up to 30% of sperm and ovum and even if it is kept in an unsuitable space for a short time before inoculation, it will disappear while, there is no place for the principle of non-existence here, and since the application of the concept of pregnancy to the embryo is true, it can be considered under Article 852 from a jurisprudential point of view (Solati, 2009, p. 118).

Chapter Two

Examination of lineage in the surrogate uterus:

2.1 First speech: Check the attribution of the child to the parents

One of the topics that is effective in explaining the nature and study of lineage in the surrogate uterus is how the child is assigned to the parents, which we follow in the paternal and maternal lineage separately.

2-1-1- How to assign a child to a father:

According to the definition of lineage in customary standards, both general and specific, medical knowledge and religious beliefs, there is no doubt that the "owner of sperm" is the father of a child born from the sperm of intercourse of his sperm with a female cell (ovum). In other words, the origin of the embryo from the father is the sperm in the man's semen, and custom, accordingly, abstracts a title called lineage to express this fact and development; In fact, the attribution to the father is based on the creation of the child from his sperm, and the man who owns the sperm is considered the father of the child.

What is known from the adjudications of the jurists also shows that a child born to a woman, in terms of paternal lineage, belongs to a man whose fetus was formed by combining his sperm with a woman's ovum, that is, if the owner of the sperm is known, he is considered as the baby 's father. Now, if his sperm is legally placed in a woman's uterus (by a valid marriage or in a suspicious manner), the law recognizes this lineage in every way. And if the placement of sperm in a woman's uterus is illegal, although the law does not recognize it, the owner of the sperm is naturally considered as the father and some traces of lineage such as the sanctity of marriage follow, and in any case the child is attributed to the man There is no other. (Mehrpour, 1997, pp. 179) The laws and laws of most countries in the world, in which the natural and real relationship is mentioned, have abstracted the title of lineage and have arranged numerous works on it, are also evidence of this claim. (Sadrzadeh Afshar, Bita, vol. 3, p. 37).

There are verses and narrations about the origin of the birth of a child from the father, briefly we will suffice to mention verse 54 of Surah Al-Furqan, in which the origin of man and the criterion of lineage are expressed in a beautiful way:

And He is the God who created everything from water and made us a family, and He is the Almighty.

The word "water" gives two possibilities:

1. Absolute water; That is, the absolute origin of living things is water.

2. Sperm; That is, man was created from sperm

The latter possibility is confirmed by the verse, "We created man from the seed of the seed of the plant, so that he may hear and see" because the context of the verse also states the same. In any case, there is a very subtle point in this verse, that is that lineage and kinship with the interpretation of forgery, which means to return and change something to a certain state, has been arranged on human beings, which by separating it from "creation human being of water". That is, the same human being created from water has a lineage, and his lineage is the validity and altered state of the water of the sperm, and does not originate from anything else.

Some legal writers, among their arguments for this theory, have referred to the jurisprudential and legal provisions about the plant.

According to the legal regulations regarding the plant, the owner of the seed, that is, the owner of the seed and the sperm, will be the owner of the plant from which it originated, even if this seed has grown and developed in another land and has borne fruit. That is, in fact, the product of a plant belongs to the owner of the sperm and seed, and the land, which is the container, bed, and carrier of that seed, has no effect on the attribution of the plant to its owner.

Article 33 of the Civil Code states: The product obtained from the land belong to the owner of the land, whether it has grown by itself or by the operations of the owner, Unless the product is either the result of a plant or a seed which belong to the other, in which case the tree and the crop will belong to the owner of the plant or seed, even if it was planted without the consent of the owner of the land.

If we dare to compare the human field with the plant and the animal, according to this theory, the genetic mother is the legal mother of the child and the surrogate mother has no relationship with the child.

From the point of view of medical knowledge, it has been proven that the origin and cell-forming embryo is the female ovum, and there is no doubt about that.

It has also been proven from the perspective that the uterus has roles, such as preparing for the acceptance of the fetus and controlling its aggressive growth, controlling and inhibiting the immune system in the uterus to prevent fetal rejection, Exchange of messages during embryo implantation and as a result of differentiation and development of undifferentiated fetal cells and formation of pairs for food, respiratory and fecal exchange of the fetus with the mother. (Ghaffari, 2008, p. 78)

2-1-2 Investigating the attribution of the child to the mother:

According to the definition of lineage in customary standards, both general and specific, medical knowledge and religious beliefs, there is no doubt that the "owner of sperm" is the father of a child born from the sperm of intercourse of his sperm with a female cell (ovum). In other words, the origin of the embryo from the father is the sperm in the man's semen, and custom, accordingly, abstracts a title called lineage to express this fact and development; In fact, the attribution to the father is based on the creation of the child from his sperm, and the man who owns the sperm is considered the father of the child.

Accordingly, several theories have been proposed on how the child is assigned to the mother:

1- Birth is the criterion for attributing a child to the mother.

2- Takun is the criterion for assigning a child to its mother.

3- The mother has two factors: birth and birth.

Commentary: Birth is the criterion for attributing a child to the mother.

Some believe that the owner of the uterus is the mother of the child. According to him, the mother's custom refers to a person who gives birth to a child, so here, too, a woman who carries a child in her womb and then gives birth to her is considered her mother. (Al-Mohseni, p. 91 / Al-Qaradawi, vol. 2, p. 197)

In proving their theory, this group of jurists states:

Basically, at the time of the revelation of the verses and the issuance of narrations, people were unaware of the new medical information that the child was the result of fertilization of sperm and egg, and considered the woman's uterus as the developing fetus, and yet the woman with the uterus was considered the mother. This shows that the basis of their judgment was childbirth; "That is, the woman who gave birth to the child was considered a mother, and the Islamic legislature also signed this custom under certain conditions." (Mohaghegh Damad, 1375, p. 2)

In other words, the issues mentioned in the language of Sharia are the home of the common understanding, and in any case, if the opinion of the holy Shari'ah is contrary to it, it will specify it. They will appear to you from their sins, from their sheep, from their sheep, except for their country and their children, and they will say that they deny the word and the force, and that God forgives their forgiveness. They are not their mothers. Their mothers are the only ones who gave birth to them, and cutting them off they say an ugly and false word, Wali (God is certainly forgiving in passing) It is in the womb! (Merghati, 2005, p. 245)

While the above verse can not be cited in this regard; Because this verse intends to abolish the ruling of zahir, which was famous among the Arab people in the time of ignorance, and to deny its effect, which was eternal sanctity. Also deny the other effect of the wife becoming a mother to the husband. (Tabatabai, 1374, vol. 19, p. 178) So the verse did not seek to express the religious meaning of "um" at all.

As it has been stated, some people argue with several verses to confirm their theory. In the words of some of the great jurists, it is stated: 1987, 2, 284).

In this noble verse, the mother is absolutely and strictly the one who gave birth to the child, and the siege here, although it is superfluous, rejects those who considered their wives as their mothers by "appearing", but it has been proven in principle. That the case is not specific or restricted and the appearance of the word is the criterion of validity for the wise (Rezania Moallem, 2001, p. 324).

Now, the question arises whether the non-specificity of the case in the verse of Zahar can be a reason to rely on it? It seems that reliance on the absolute is valid only where the speaker is in a position to express all the conditions and conditions so that "lack of expression in the position of expression" is a reason for the absolute.

Chapter Three

Civil rights of the child derived from a rented womb and the characteristics of the rented womb contract:

The goal of the ability to enjoy is the ability to have the right, and for this reason, for the living human being, legal personality and rights and duties are considered, and after being born, she has the right and the duty. With these descriptions, the legislator considers rights for the fetus according to his interests. Article 957 of the Civil Code stipulates: "The fetus has civil rights provided when he is born alive." Establishment of the rights is conditional on live birth and it is discovered that from the time of fertilization and during the embryonic period, he had this ability to have the right. There is no doubt about the acquisition of these rights for the fetus resulting from artificial insemination Since its clotting in the womb and also the fetus from in vitro fertilization Since its transfer to the uterus.

3-1 First speech: Civil rights of the child resulting from rented womb:

the title of pregnancy, which is also the subject of having rights in narrations, jurisprudence and laws, is also true. Some refer to pregnancy as the embryo that is growing inside the uterus and the title of the combined sperm is not valid as long as it is outside the uterus. In other words, pregnancy is considered to be the mixing of a live fertilized ovum with a living tissue, and with this definition, the zygote formed outside the uterus is also subject to pregnancy, and as a result, it will also be subject to the Shari'a rules. (Asif Mohseni, 1998, vol. 1, p. 97)

Of course, this view is also endorsed by some other jurists, who say, "Man is potential, even though he is in the developmental stage outside the womb." Shahidi, 2002, p. 171)

3-1-1- Eligibility of a person to have the right:

The purpose of the ability to enjoy is the ability to have the right, and for this reason, for the living human being, legal personality and rights and duties are considered, and after being born, she has the right and the duty. With these descriptions, the legislator considers rights for the fetus according to his interests. Article 957 of the Civil Code stipulates: "The fetus has civil rights provided when he is born alive." Establishment of the rights is conditional on live birth and it is discovered that from the time of fertilization and during the embryonic period, he had this ability to have the right. There is no doubt about the acquisition of these rights for the fetus resulting from artificial insemination Since its clotting in the womb and also the fetus from in vitro fertilization Since its transfer to the uterus.

Because the title of pregnancy, which is also the subject of having rights in narrations, jurisprudence and laws, is also true. Some refer to pregnancy as the embryo that is growing inside the uterus and the title of the combined sperm is not valid as long as it is outside the uterus. In other words, pregnancy is considered to be the mixing of a live fertilized ovum with a living tissue, and with this definition, the zygote formed outside the uterus is also subject to pregnancy, and as a result, it will also be subject to the Shari'a rules. (Asif Mohseni, 1998, vol. 1, p. 97)

Of course, this view is also endorsed by some other jurists, who say, "Man is potential, even though he is in the developmental stage outside the womb." Shahidi, 2002, p. 171)

3-1-2- The validity of the will on the child obtained from the rented womb:

Another right that can be recounted for a child born in a rented womb is the right to be a legatee, and this right can apparently also be considered for a fetus resulting from IVF. Because the only condition of the will is the presence of the legatee at the time of the will, and this is while the existence of the fetus is that its sperm was coagulated at that time whether this coagulation is in the laboratory or in the uterus. The question now is whether the will is valid for frozen embryos in the laboratory or not? In response, it should be stated that the application of Article 850 of the Civil Code requires that the legatee must be present and be able to own what has been bequeathed to him. On the other hand, Article 851 states that "a will is valid for the fetus, but its possession is conditional on its being born alive." Therefore, being born alive can be considered as a criterion of possession. It should be noted that the law does not even consider abortion as a criterion for the decline of possession because it considers the fetus eligible to have rights. Therefore, Article 852 states: "If the fetus is aborted as a result of a crime, the legatee has the right to inherit it, unless the crime prevents inheritance." On the other hand, some jurists apply the principle of non-existence of this embryo formed in the laboratory environment, because in vitro fertilization and freezing cause the destruction of up to 30% of sperm and ovum and even if it is kept in an unsuitable space for a short time before inoculation, it will disappear while, there is no place for the principle of non-existence here, and since the application of the concept of pregnancy to the embryo is true, it can be considered under Article 852 from a jurisprudential point of view (Solati, 2009, p. 118).

3-1-3 - Having devotion:

As stated, the fetus is eligible to have the right and to enjoy civil rights and has legal personality, and this can be deduced from the statement of Article 957 of the Civil Code which said "The fetus enjoys civil rights provided it is born alive." On the other hand, Article 49 states that "the expenses necessary for the maintenance of the property which is for profit are not borne by the beneficiary, unless otherwise stipulated." Article 69 also considers devotion as a kind of usufruct and states that "devotion on the extinct is not valid except in the existing consequence" and therefore it can be concluded that devotion on frozen embryos is also considered valid.

3-1-4- Having donee:

According to the legislator in Article 957 of the Civil Code, "the fetus enjoys civil rights provided that it is born alive" so the fetus from a rented womb can also receive a donee because donee is a free possession in favor of the child and there is no reason for not accepting it.

3-1-5- Confession in favor of the fetus:

Article 1270 of the Civil Code states that "a confession in favor of the fetus is effective if it is born alive." Therefore, it can be stated that by applying the fetus to the laboratory embryo, he can be considered to have the right to confess in his favor.

3-1-6- Right to inherit from parents:

Another right that can be considered for the fetus is to inherit from its parents like a born child, of course, Article 957 of the Civil Code states that "the fetus enjoys civil rights provided it is born alive and we also applied the embryo to the laboratory fetus, so it can be subject to Article 875 of the Civil Code which states "The condition of inheritance is to be alive at the time of the heir's death, and if there is an embryo, it inherits if its sperm was coagulated at the time of death and is born alive, although it dies immediately after birth.".

According to Article 878 of the Civil Code "If, at the time of the heir's death, there is a fetus which, if it can be born hereditary, prevents the inheritance of all or some of the other heirs, the division of the inheritance will not take place until it is known, and if the fetus does not prevent the inheritance of any of the other heirs. If they want to divide the estate, they must set aside a share for the fetus that is equal to the share of two sons from the same inheritance class, and the share of each heir is reserved until the status of the fetus is determined."

3-1-7- Custody:

Custody in the literal sense means take someone under one's wing, and in legal reform it is to take care of one's wife and children, and custody in a sense means to take care of, nurture and educate him/her. Although the Civil Code does not provide a definition of custody, the issue of custody and upbringing of children is addressed in Articles 1168 to 1179 of the Civil Code and Articles 40 to 47 of the fifth chapter of the new Family Protection Law. The concept of custody is different from guardianship because guardianship means the power and authority that the law gives to the father and paternal grandfather to manage the child's affairs (including the administration of property and finances) to act in the best interests of the child. This right can be transferred after death by will. The Supreme Court, in its decision No. 4236 dated 1/20/73, ruled: "Considering that custody is both a right and a duty according to the law, the right can be revoked, but the duty cannot be revoked and compromised."

3-1-8- Not intimate and sanctity of marriage:

Article 1045 of the Civil Code prohibits intermarriage with relatives – affinity or blood relatives- to some extent and said that "Marriage to the following relatives is forbidden, even if the relationship is the result of suspicion or adultery:

- Marriage with fathers and grandfathers and with mother and grandparents as much as it goes up in inheritance classes

- Marriage with children as much as it goes down in inheritance classes.

- Marriage with brothers and sisters and their children as far as it goes down in inheritance classes.

- Marriage with one's uncles and aunts and uncles and aunts of parents and ancestors in inheritance classes

Therefore, the owner of the ovum and sperm, since they are the real mother and father of the fetus, marriage with them is forbidden, but the question is how the fetus donated from the sperm bank is related to the owner of the uterus and his wife, which is discussed here. Some jurists believe that this woman and her child born from her womb do not have a special ruling because she has no genetic connection with the owner of the uterus except after birth when the owner of the uterus breastfeeds her and equal to Article 1046, he/her becomes to be foster intimate. This article said that foster relationship in terms of the sanctity of marriage is considered affinity relationship, provided that:

First – the breast milk is obtained from legitimate pregnancy

Second – Milk is sucked directly from the breast.

Third – the baby should be breastfed at least overnight or 15 times in a row without eating any other food or milk.

Fourth – The baby should be breastfed before the end of two years from his birth.

Fifth – the amount of milk a child eats are of one couple.

Therefore, if a child eats some milk of one woman and some milk of another woman during the day and night, it will not be forbidden, even if the husband of the two women is the same. Also, if a woman has a foster daughter and son who have breastfed each of them from the milk of the other husband, that boy or girl is not a foster brother and sister, and marriage between them is not forbidden in this regard.

3-2 Second speech:

The Islamic Consultative Assembly approved the law on the method of donating embryos to infertile couples on 2003/08/05 and since then, embryo transfer and uterine rent have been subject to the law. For the first time, this law discusses centers that undertake the transfer and maintenance of embryos, and Article 1 of this law stipulates that according to this law, all competent specialized infertility treatment centers will be allowed, in compliance with the sharia rules of the conditions set forth in this law. Transfer embryos resulting from ectopic insemination of legal and religious couples after the written consent of the fetal couple to the uterus of women whose infertility has been proven after marriage and undergoing medical procedures (either alone or both).

According to the fatwas of Ayatollah Khomeini, Fazel Lankarani, Makarem Shirazi, Khoei, Safi Golpayegani, the principle of embryo formation from religious and legal couples with observance of religious aspects and lack of forbidden provisions is permissible, and there is no doubt in the correctness of the principle, but if with forbidden provisions Some, such as Imam Khomeini, believe in its absolute sanctity, and others, such as Makarem Shirazi, Sistani, and Fazel Lankarani, consider it permissible in cases of distress and necessity, and the meaning of disturbing rulings is cases that disrupt marital life or a woman's illness. The likes of it can be enumerated In Article 2, the request to receive a donated embryo must be prepared jointly by the couple and submitted to the court, and the court will issue a permit to receive the embryo if the following conditions are met: a. The wife has the ability to receive the fetus. B) Couples have moral competence. C- None of the couples are estranged. D- None of the couples suffer from incurable diseases. 5. None of the couples are addicted to drugs. F- Couples must have the citizenship of the Islamic Republic of Iran.

Of course, some jurists, such as Muhammad al-Qa'ini al-Mabsut fi al-Fiqh al-Maasir, in the chapter "Medical Issues" regarding the sanctity of touch, have stated that the evidences of sanctity refer to the external organs of the body and do not include the internal organs of the human body and internal environments. Since the uterus is one of these internal environments, we have no reason to sanctify it. Health and medical education should be allowed because with this supervision, transmission of diseases and interbreeding can be prevented to a large extent. The premise is that this is also true, for example, the method of masturbation should not be used to ejaculate semen, or there should be no haram act in transferring it to the wife's uterus, such as body touch or opinion (Marandi, 2008, p. 12). And a child born in terms of care, upbringing, alimony and respect It is like the duties and responsibilities of children and parents. And the fetal donor will not have the right to custody of the newborn.

According to Article 3 of the above-mentioned law, the duties and responsibilities of the couple receiving the fetus and the child born in terms of maintenance, education, alimony and respect are the same as the duties and responsibilities of the children and parents; In the first way, between the couple receiving the fetus and the child born, the sanctity of marriage is created like a natural child, and in terms of inheritance rules, it will be the same as a natural child, ie all inheritance laws and regulations will apply to him, because permission is in the object. Permission will also be in the supplies of the object, and when insemination, which is the sanctity of marriage, inheritance, etc., must also be accepted. If the request to receive the embryo is joint, it should be stated that in the current court process, the applicant couple should write their name as the plaintiff in the petition column and determine the issuance of the embryo transfer permit as a petition in the petition column and submit the petition to the competent court.

The family submits. Obviously, the above petition also includes the formal provision of the petition in accordance with the Code of Civil Procedure. It is not possible for couples to have children, which means that it is up to the court to determine that couples cannot have other methods of pregnancy, such as IVF injection into the cytoplasm of sperm, intrauterine insemination of sperm, and transfer of the egg or eggs into the fallopian tube. Falubs cannot conceive with their sperm and eggs. And, of course, the wife should have the ability to keep the fetus, so in the current procedure of forensic medicine, the above conditions are met (Amirkian, 2015, p. 86). And non-confirmation of the couple's eligibility can be appealed. Moral competence of the couple is a condition for maintaining the norm and mental health and upbringing of the child. Regarding the attainment of this competence, the competent authority is the judge, and it should be stated that he can attain it in any way, and his knowledge is sufficient for this attainment, whether considering his appearance and background or researching the work and residence of couples and others.Ways to achieve this knowledge. It seems inconsistent and somewhat inconsis...Executive regulations of the law on how to donate embryos to infertile couples.

Definitions and generalities of the article

1- In this regulation, the following words and terms are used in the detailed meanings related to:

A- Law: The law refers to the method of donating embryos to infertile couples approved in 2003.

B- Embryo: The sperm resulting from ectopic insemination is a legal and religious couple that will be from the reproductive stage to a maximum of five days. This fetus can be both fresh and frozen.

C- Embryo donation: Voluntary and free transfer of one or more embryos from eligible couples stipulated in the law and this regulation, to authorized specialized infertility treatment centers for transfer to the applicant couples with the conditions stipulated in the law.

- Conditions for donating and receiving embryos

Article 2 - Donor couples must have the following conditions.

A- Interest and relationship between legal and sharia marriage

B- Normal physical and mental health and appropriate IQ.

C- Not addicted to addictive and psychotropic substances.

D- Not suffering from incurable diseases such as AIDS, hepatitis, etc.

Note: Authorized specialized infertility treatment centers are obliged to prove the existence of the conditions mentioned in this article before receiving the fetus from the donors.

Article 3 - Embryo donation must be done with the written consent of the donor couples and in authorized specialized infertility treatment centers, with their identification and confidentiality.

Article 4 - Couples applying for donated embryos must meet the conditions set forth in Article 2 of the law.

Article 5 - The request to receive a donated embryo will be considered in a competent court and out of turn, without observing the formalities of civil procedure. The issuance of an order rejecting the application and not approving the eligibility of the couple can be appealed.

- Duties and duties of authorized infertility treatment centers

Article 6- Authorized specialized centers for infertility treatment are obliged to take action in the following cases:

A- Keeping donated embryos by Muslim and non-Muslim donors separately and observing the religious and religious fit of the applicant couple with the donated embryo at the time of transfer.

B- Receiving and keeping the cross-sectional decision of the judicial authority from the applicant.

C- Issuance of the necessary certificate and letter of introduction based on the confirmation of physical and mental health for the applicants for receiving the fetus according to the provisions of the law and this regulation.

D- Receiving, storing and transferring donated embryos in completely confidential conditions Note- Information related to donated embryos is classified as general information.

Article 7- The certificate of inability to conceive and also the ability of the wife to receive and maintain the fetus, after conducting detailed medical tests and examinations, is within the competence of authorized specialized infertility treatment centers.

Necessary conditions for receiving, storing and transferring embryos:

Article 8- Each of the authorized specialized centers for infertility treatment can establish a fetal bank according to the instructions of the Ministry of Health, Treatment and Medical Education. This bank is responsible for receiving, maintaining and transferring embryos to infertile couples in accordance with the provisions of the law and these regulations.

Article 9- The Transplant Management Center of the Ministry of Health, Treatment and Medical Education is obliged to exercise strict supervision over the receipt, maintenance and transfer of embryos in accordance with the instructions of the said Ministry.

Article 10- Submitting documents and information related to donors and recipients of donated embryos is allowed only in compliance with the laws related to the protection of state secrets and to the competent judicial authorities.

3-3 Third speech: court decision:

Regarding the petition of Mr. P. and Ms. Z to request the issuance of a sentence and a license for embryo donation, according to the comprehensive case file and according to the marriage document No. 468-8 / 9 issued by the city office, the relationship of permanent marriage is established and by providing documents and certificates Medicine dated 2/16 of Noon Hospital stated that they did not have children during their ten years of marriage and their infertility was confirmed. According to the answer No. 55/1 / 3333- 3/22, after the necessary examinations, the above was confirmed and other investigations of the court confirm the moral competence and mental and physical health of the couple and the history of drug and opium addiction and other criminal records. They were not observed.

The court found the request of the above-mentioned to be fixed and acceptable, and according to the law on donating embryos to infertile couples, approved by the Islamic Consultative Assembly on 4/29/2003, the said couples are allowed from the legal and specialized centers Receive legal and sharia. The duties and responsibilities of couples donating the recipient of the fetus and the child born in terms of maintenance and upbringing and alimony and respect are the same duties and responsibilities of children and parents.

Theory: Embryo donation is eligible for applicants, including non-drug addiction, non-incurable disease, especially carrier and infectious, which is dangerous for the fetus and pregnant mother, and genetically predisposed to fertility after testing, which requires legal prescription. It is issued by the courts after referral and inquiry from forensic medicine.

3-4 Fourth speech: Characteristics of rental uterus contract:

In the present speech, we will examine the alternative uterus contract according to the terms of the contract (consent or ceremonial) in terms of the effects of the contract (necessary or permissible) and according to the economic subject and purpose (free, negligent and transactional) to determine this Types of contracts in the slogan of which of these divisions.

3-4-1 Satisfaction or formality of the surrogate contract:

Contract in terms of free or conditional creativity of the will is divided into three types of intentions (consent, ceremonial and objective) (Shahidi, 2007, vol. 1, p. 84).

A consent contract is a contract that, if the basic and specific conditions of the transaction are met, is formed only with the common intention of the parties, provided it is expressed and without the need for anything else. In contrast, a formal contract is a contract that, in addition to the consent of the parties and the expression of their common intention for the occurrence of this contract, it is necessary to observe certain formalities determined by the legislator; For example: the sale of real estate in Iranian law is a ceremonial contract because: in addition to the common intention of the parties requires the preparation of an official document. An objective contract is also a contract whose occurrence is subject to the surrender of the subject of commitment or possession.

Inferred from Articles 190 and 191 of the Civil Code, it is understood that in order to conclude a contract, the existence of the intention to sign and the basic conditions set forth in Article 190 of the Civil Code are sufficient, and agreement is both a necessary element for concluding a contract and other formalities. It is not necessary. (Shahidi; Katozian, 2007, pp. 36 and 137).

Therefore, it can be said that in our law, the principle is the satisfaction of contracts and the contract is made by compromise and does not need any special form. Therefore, in the case of an alternative uterus contract, which has a nature similar to a person's lease contract, it should also be considered as a consent contract. However, due to the importance of the subject of such contracts and its very important effects, for better protection of the family, special form and certain formalities to express the agreement of the two wills and the conditions for concluding such contracts should be determined to be among the ceremonial contracts.

At first glance, it seems that the uterine contract is an alternative to a consent contract; Because: in our law, the principle should be the satisfaction of contracts. In the case of this contract, the legislator has not determined any formalities, so based on the principle of consent of the contracts, the contract of alternative uterus can be considered as a consent contract. However, it seems that the surrogacy contract is so important that the legislator should consider the writtenness or even the formality of such a contract as one of the conditions for its validity in order to prevent future disputes and conflicts that will have very negative effects. To facilitate its proof and regulate it by the competent legal authority and monitor the existence of special conditions of this contract (Collective of Authors, 2007, p. 372)

On the other hand, it should be noted that any woman with any blood and relative relationship with the couple requesting a child, can not replace the uterus as a surrogate mother, for example: the mother of the wife can not sperm-induced fetus Carry the groom and his daughter's eggs; Because: According to the majority of Shiite jurists, citing the analogy, the priority of a child born from a surrogate womb is considered as a foster child or as a foster child (Safaei, 2003, p. 222).

As a result, since in Imami jurisprudence, breastfeeding, if it takes place after marriage, has the same effect as before marriage and invalidates the previous marriage, the action of the wife's mother in this act leads to the invalidity of the infertile couple's marriage, which Opposite is the main purpose of resorting to surrogacy in pregnancy. Because a brother's child is considered a husband or wife with a foster sister, and a person cannot have a marriage relationship with his or her foster sister. The same should be said of other people who cannot be married due to breastfeeding.

The conclusion of an alternative uterine contract is also subject to the fulfillment of the legal and personal conditions of the parties. For example, couples must be infertile (this condition is the responsibility of a reputable doctor or the surrogate mother must have had a pregnancy experience (at least once). It seams.

Explain that, as a result, if the contract of succession in pregnancy with the above arguments has the nature of a lease contract, it is obvious that it should be considered as a consent contract; Because in the will, the rent of persons, the agreement of two wills, is a necessary and sufficient element to close it; Therefore, it happens by mutual consent and does not require any special form. However, it seems that due to the importance of this contract and the very important effects that arise from such a contract on lineage, inheritance and privacy, as well as the secondary condition and often therapeutic aspect of this method of pregnancy, it is necessary to maintain more and better family protection. , The special form and certain formalities to express the agreement of the two wills are valid so that the said contract is among the ceremonial contracts and another exception is considered as the exceptions of the principle of consent of the contracts; In order to be able to oversee the preparation and conclusion of such contracts.

Certain forms and formalities can include certain medical examinations to confirm the infertility of a parent or applicant, to verify the physical health of the surrogate mother and her ability to conceive, to obtain the necessary medical permits from reputable medical centers, to monitor the procedures of certain centers and to register , Events and how to set conditions in the contract.

3-4-2 Necessary or permissible replacement uterine contract:

The contract is divided into necessary, permissible and optional contracts in terms of the degree of obligation that both parties have in maintaining their contract. A contract is a contract in which neither party to the transaction has the right to terminate that law, except as otherwise provided by the legislature, in other words, all contracts are required except as permitted by law. The necessary contract can be dissolved only by one of the options or with the consent of the parties, in contrast to the contract is a contract that can always be terminated by law and the optional contract is a necessary contract in which one of the There are options.

Regarding the surrogate contract, he said: "This contract, due to the need to protect the fetus and protect its rights, requires that it be a necessary contract and the parties do not have the right to break it." Because the principle of the necessity of contracts, which in Article 219 AH. It has been mentioned, confirming the fact that private contracts, except for what the law stipulates their permissibility, are binding between the parties and the possibility of terminating the contract is exceptional and contrary to the principle (Katozian, 1993, Vol. 1, p. 39)

Therefore, all private contracts, except those specified in the law itself, should be considered as necessary contracts.

As a result, the surrogate uterus contract is a necessary contract in this regard, and the parties must abide by the obligations set forth in this contract and fulfill them.

Also, one of the requirements of the marriage contract is its dissolution due to death, insanity and idiot of one of the parties, while the belief in the dissolution of the alternative uterus contract in these cases is contrary to the rights of the child and public order. (Katozian, 2006, p. 23)

The contract is also not enforced in this contract due to opposition to public order because: Due to the importance of the issue of surrogacy in pregnancy and respect for the rights of the child, we can not give the right to terminate or contract the contract for one or both parties. But on the other hand, due to the importance of the surrogate mother and her heartfelt satisfaction in this contract, and due to the best interests of the child, this contract can be considered permissible before and after pregnancy. Do not consider the contract as a suspended contract, because: in this case, the desired result is obtained as a result of the suspension of the contract on the pregnancy itself, and believing in this opinion will not be of any use.

3-4-3 Ownership or covenant of an alternative uterus contract:

An ownership contract, as its name implies, is a contract whose direct result is the transfer of ownership, and a contractual contract is a contract that merely gives rise to an obligation and obligation on the part of the contractor or causes the transfer and termination of the obligation. (Shahidi, 2004, vol. 1, p. 83; Katozian, 2007, p. 34; Jafari Langroudi, 2005, pp. 457 - 459)

According to the above definitions, there is no surrogate in the mother's contract, and such contracts create an obligation for each of the parties, so the uterine lease contract with the surrogate mother is included in the division of test contracts.

3-4-4- Alternative or free replacement uterine contract:

A reciprocal contract is a contract that has two items, each of which is in exchange for the other. These two items may be both property or both obligations or one property and the other obligation. But a contract that has a case and has no exchange is called a free or non-exchange contract.

As mentioned in all types of surrogate mother contracts, these contracts may be of the exchange type (commercial) or of the non-exchange type and friendly (non-commercial) type. Therefore, a contract that is done in the form of compensation is a type of exchange contracts and the effects of these contracts are borne on it.

On the other hand, if the contract that is concluded is non-commercial and altruistic, it is considered as a free contract. In these contracts, the main purpose of the parties is not to gain material benefits and exchange property, but the specific emotions are the main motivator in accepting the obligation and are usually concluded between close relatives. Of course, it should be known that in non-exchange contracts, a condition can be changed and this condition does not change the nature of the original contract from non-exchange to compensation. (Katozian, 2007, pp. 28 and 29)

In view of the above, it is very clear that the uterine contract is a commercial alternative to the contract of exchange, because the obligation of the surrogate mother is in this respect against the obligation of the parents, and their common intention is to exchange the two.

In contrast, the altruistic alternative to the contract of the uterus is a non-compensatory contract, because in this case the surrogate mother, without considering economic considerations and only in terms of moral, emotional and humanitarian issues, assumes an obligation to the parents, while In return, there is no obligation on his part from the parents.

In the altruistic surrogate parent contract, the parents charge a sum of money in the contract to pay the necessary costs, which can be considered a condition for a change in the gratuitous contract. As we know, the existence of a condition of change in a non-compensable contract does not replace it, because this condition has a sub-face. Therefore, altruistic alternative uterine contract is in the group of non-compensatory contracts. (Naebzadeh, 2001, p. 103)

Some have argued that the existence of a monetary relationship in a pregnancy surrogacy contract is appropriate, stating that this incentive has negative consequences, for example, altruistic motives in this regard disappear and lead to the commercialization of such a contract. It also makes this contract a tool for the exploitation and financial exploitation of women and establishes something against human dignity (Group of Authors, 2007, p. 178), therefore, they believe that every amount should be paid properly. Absolutely or in addition to the costs and damages in the contract of replacement of the uterus is prohibited (Ibid., P. 117).

This concern may be present and understandable, but such an issue is not limited to surrogacy in pregnancy, if surrogacy is prohibited for this reason, why not prohibit other types of women's services in society, such as maid service, child care and ... Is this kind of work compatible with human dignity? (Rezania Moallem, 2004, p. 278).

Opposition to the payment of money and the prohibition of commercial alternative uterine contracts are also incorrect; Because in that case, some people can be persuaded to volunteer with flattering language, and this will be more beneficial. In addition, refusing to pay for the use of another respectable job is immoral. Also, refusing to pay the surrogate mother does not seem fair, and it is not considered a logical response to the goodness of the surrogate mother, who suffers many hardships as a result of pregnancy.This prohibition may prevent people from substituting in pregnancy and have a deterrent role in this regard, and in practice, infertile couples are deprived of such a method to solve infertility problems.

On the other hand, some studies show that more than 60% of surrogate volunteers did not do so only because of their financial situation and earning money, but also because of spiritual and moral reasons. In other words, although material motives are important, they are not the first motive (Jamei Authors, 2007, p. 372).

As most jurists (Shahidi, 2003, p. 217) and jurists have agreed to pay wages to the surrogate mother and compare this situation with the hiring of a woman to breastfeed another child, if, this action is explicitly prescribed in Islamic jurisprudence . The result is that an altruistic surrogate contract is a non-exchange contract and a commercial contract is a trade-off.

3-4-5 The negligence or transactionality of the replacement uterus contract:

According to the legal regulations regarding the plant, the owner of the seed, that is, the owner of the seed and the sperm, will be the owner of the plant from which it originated, even if this seed has grown and developed in another land and has borne fruit. That is, in fact, the product of a plant belongs to the owner of the sperm and seed, and the land, which is the container, bed, and carrier of that seed, has no effect on the attribution of the plant to its owner.

Article 33 of the Civil Code states: The product obtained from the land belong to the owner of the land, whether it has grown by itself or by the operations of the owner, Unless the product is either the result of a plant or a seed which belong to the other, in which case the tree and the crop will belong to the owner of the plant or seed, even if it was planted without the consent of the owner of the land.

If we dare to compare the human field with the plant and the animal, according to this theory, the genetic mother is the legal mother of the child and the surrogate mother has no relationship with the child.

From the point of view of medical knowledge, it has been proven that the origin and cell-forming embryo is the female ovum, and there is no doubt about that.

3-5 Fifth statement: Conditions for the validity of the surrogate contract:

According to the civil law of our country, the conditions for concluding any contract in accordance with Article 190 of this law are determined as follows:

1) Intention of the parties and their consent

2) The competence of the parties

3) The specific subject to be traded

4) Legitimacy for the transaction

Therefore, according to the above article, the replacement uterus contract must also have the above four conditions in order to have legal validity. Now, except for the fourth condition, which, based on the acceptance of the validity of such a contract, we examine each of the above conditions while complying with the replacement uterine contract.

3-5-1 Existence of intention and consensus of the parties:

Intention and consent are necessary in each other's contract, and without each of them, the contract is not complete and correct. Satisfaction alone does not lead to writing and has no effect on the world of law, nor will an intention that is not based on real consent be fully effective. (Katozian, 2007, p. 53)

In the alternative uterus contract, the parties agree with each other after the intention and consent to perform the operation. In such contracts, the intention of each party is quite clear, because this contract is one of the special contracts and, like other contracts, it is not possible for a mistake to be made in the intended intention. Because it is very unlikely that the parties will not be aware of each other's intention to do so, the main element in the contract to use a surrogate uterus, "intent and consent," is fully realized.

3-5-2 The competence of the parties in the alternative uterus contract:

The competence of the parties in the contract of surrogacy in Iranian law, a person is considered a person when he can both have the right legally (the ability to enjoy) and can exercise the right. (Ability to resign based on the opinion of jurists); (Shahid I, 1381, p. 180) and according to Article 211 of the Civil Code, in order for the interlocutors to be considered natives, they must be mature, wise and rational. In the contract for the use of a woman's uterus, in addition to the fact that the parties to the contract must be wise, mature and mature (general competence), other conditions are also required (special competence) that doctors consider to prevent possible problems. Although we do not have a specific law or procedure in this regard, we can mention the special competence of infertility of the applicant couple, the pregnancy of the woman who has a uterus, the consent of the husband if the uterus has a husband, and so on.

3-5-3 The subject of the transaction in the replacement uterus contract:

Basically, in any marriage, its subject must be clear and definite. Article 214 of the Civil Code states: "The subject of the transaction must be property or an act which each of the parties to the transaction undertakes to surrender or perform." In contracts where the surrogate contract is in this group, the parties undertake to do something. Thus, in the mother's contract, the successor to the transaction, or "the subject of the obligation," is to do the work. Therefore, it is necessary for this action to be specific for each of them.

3-6 Sixth speech: Comparing the contract of surrogate uterus with other contracts:

In this section, we examine the replacement uterus contract with other contracts to determine whether the replacement uterus contract will be included in this type of contract, in other words, it depends on one or more of these contracts or will be an independent contract.

3-6-1 Alternative uterine contract and sale contract:

Some Arabic-speaking jurists have ruled that the womb contract invalidates the contract, believing that it replaces the nature of the contract of sale and sale of the child born of it. Because in this contract, the subject (child) was not present at the time of the contract, also the characteristics of the seller are not specified at the time of the contract. (Mahmoud Hamzeh, 2007, p. 315)

Other Arab jurists have argued that the sale of human beings is not permissible because human beings are not property so that they can be the subject of sale (Al-Fayadh, 2001, p. 26).

Even some Iranian jurists have considered the surrogacy contract as a child-rearing contract, arguing that "all aspects of life creation should be limited to the couple, and any third-party interference is reprehensible and rejected, because the spouse The biological and spiritual views are united and the child-building contract is a violation of this union "(Katozian, 2006, vol. 2, p. 36)

In response to the above statements, it can be said: In this way, infertile couples do not buy the child, the child is their biological child and is genetically related to them, and no one can buy something that belongs to him. In addition, what determines the nature of a contract is the common intention of the parties, while in a surrogate uterine contract, the infertile couple agrees with the surrogate mother to conceive, carry, and deliver their own fetus. In addition, the theory of the sale of the uterine contract replaces the belief that the owner of the uterus is the real mother of the child, while according to most Shiite jurists and jurists, the real mother in this contract is the owner of the egg.

Also, according to the principle of correctness stated in Article 223 of the Civil Code, in the case where the words contract have different meanings in custom, the phrase should be carried to a meaning that is considered a valid contract (Katozian, 1374, vol. 2, p. 500). The surrogate womb is also valid according to most jurists, so its nature must be interpreted in such a way that the contract is considered valid. One of the reasons that can be stated on the distinction between a contract of sale and a contract of alternative uterus is that the contract of sale is a proprietary and exchangeable contract, while the uterine contract is a substitute contract and is only in some cases a commercial type of exchange. Also, the subject of the contract of sale must be specific or general, while the subject of the uterine contract replaces the obligation to care for and nurture the fetus, and in this contract there is no objective ownership.

3-6-2 Alternate uterus contract with lease contract of persons and objects:

Some jurists have considered the surrogate contract as a kind of rental agreement; Because: In terms of nature, among certain contracts, the most similar contract to a surrogate contract is a lease contract (a group of authors, 2007, p. 437).

The similarity of a person's lease with an alternative womb contract is that the person (hirer) in the lease contract undertakes to own a certain interest or benefit from the tenant for a certain period of time or for a certain rent, or is obliged to Do a certain wage to do a certain job for the tenant (Katozian, 1998, p. 557).

In the contract of surrogacy, the surrogate mother also undertakes to become pregnant for a certain fee using assisted reproduction methods and the fetus belonging to infertile couples or third parties, and to bear the fetus in her womb after the pregnancy and after delivery. Deliver the newborn baby to the parents. Some European authors have pointed out that ambiguity in the nature of the surrogate contract is one of the obstacles to the implementation of this contract, and acknowledged that the uterine contract replaces the nature of a personal service contract (a kind of rent).

If we consider the contract of surrogacy as the nature of the lease of persons, the other drawbacks to the ability of the uterus to lease can no longer be challenged here; Because: According to jurists, renting persons is a contractual contract (Katouzian, 2008, vol. 1, pp. 567 and 568), and ownership is made in it and only the person undertakes to do the current for a certain period of time for a certain salary. If the labor law also considers the labor contract, which is a kind of rent of persons, as a contractual contract (Article 20 of the labor law)

Despite the above, some people do not consider the lease agreement suitable for the issue of surrogacy in pregnancy and have argued for its incompatibility, and believe that the regulatory agreement in this regard, because it can not be analyzed in the form of certain contracts, is inevitable. It is placed in the line of indefinite contracts (Jafarzadeh, 1993, p. 73, Naebzadeh, 1997, p. 255).

For example, it has been argued that if we consider the human labor force to be a benefit, the benefit is the subject of the surrogate mother's contract. In addition, being the owner of such a benefit means that the surrogate mother is the owner and no one can own a person according to the contract (Naebzadeh, 2001, p. 156).

This argument does not seem to be appropriate for the incompatibility of a person's rental relationship with the issue of surrogacy in pregnancy, because it is a matter of the benefit of the human labor force, as well as the fact that renting a person is a type of rent and a person can benefit from it. It is accepted in Iranian jurisprudence and law and there is no difference in it (Katouzian, 1999,p 204). Hiring a woman to breastfeed a baby, in other words a breastfeeding contract, is one of the good examples that can be cited in this regard. This example also fits in well with the discussion of succession in pregnancy. Such a contract states that it is permissible to hire a woman to satisfy, while the benefit of the subject of surrogacy in breastfeeding is "the natural function of the breastfeeding mother's breast in milk production" and this benefit is also part of the existence and personality of the breastfeeding mother.

Another point is that the ownership of such a special benefit from the surrogate mother does not mean that she is the owner, because the lease of the contracted persons is a contract and no ownership is made in it, so the tenant is not hired in this contract.

In addition, if the impediments to using a rental contract for the subject of surrogacy in pregnancy include "being part of the personal interest of the surrogate mother's benefit" and "ownership of the surrogate mother for such benefit", this is the case for other definite or indefinite contracts.There will also be a sentence that seeks to attribute such a benefit to the parents. The result is that with such arguments we must invalidate the principle of the contract of surrogacy with any nature, because it is not possible for other contracts to take this benefit out of the scope of a person's personality and change its nature.

On the other hand, according to Article 466 of the Civil Code, a lease is a contract according to which the tenant becomes the owner of the same interests as the lessee. According to the jurists (Mousavi Khomeini, 1984, p. 575) and Article 466 of the Civil Code, the landlord owns the rental benefits to the tenant. From now on, the tenant is the owner and, like him, enjoys the same benefits. (Katozian, 1993, vol. 1, p. 361) According to Article 476 of the Civil Code, the landlord must hand over the same tenant to the tenant, and submission under Article 477 of the same law must be in a situation where the tenant can make good use of it. On the other hand, since the withdrawal of benefits depends on the surrender of the same tenant, so its surrender by the landlord is necessary, and it is clear that the surrogate mother can not surrender her organs "womb" to the real parents. As a result, according to the above, the contract for the use of a surrogate uterus cannot be considered in accordance with the lease of objects. But in comparison with the rent of persons, it should be said that the rent of persons is a contract according to which the tenant becomes the owner of the hired interests. In this respect, the lease of a contracted person is the property and by it the interests of the hired person are exchanged in a certain place. (Ibid., P. 567) But the benefit of the surrogate mother's contract is the natural function of the uterus in fetal development. This benefit is part of the character of the surrogate mother, and real parents cannot own this benefit. Also, if we consider the surrogate mother's contract as a rental contract, the benefit, which is the natural function of the surrogate mother's uterus in fetal development, takes on a financial form, so that the surrogate mother has the right to demand a sum of money for it.

However, these rights are part of the rights of the personality and have no financial face. Therefore, it seems that contrary to the opinion of some who consider the structure of a person's lease contract to be an appropriate structure with the agreement and commitment of a surrogate in pregnancy (Hamdollahi; Roshan, 2009, 146)

The benefit of the surrogate mother's contract is not such that it can be put in the form of a lease, and we consider the payment of money to the surrogate mother in the way that the lease treats it. But there are two major drawbacks to the theory of renting persons as an alternative uterine contract. In renting persons, the delivery of the benefit is done by doing the work, the subject of the obligation and the delivery of the manufactured goods, and if the subject of the obligation is lost before that, the hired person has no right to wages (Katozian, 1993, vol. 1, p. 421) In the case of a surrogate mother, if the child is aborted before birth, the surrogate mother cannot be considered entitled to pay according to the rules of rent, because she has fulfilled her obligation to take care of the fetus and achieve the intended result. It is beyond his power, moreover, it does not seem fair that the surrogate mother does not deserve to be paid in this case, despite the great hardship she has endured in this way.

Secondly, the surrogate contract consists of a set of obligations, so that not all of these obligations can be considered as a result of a person's lease. In other words, by analyzing the provisions of the surrogate uterus contract, it is concluded that only a part of its obligations can be related to the rent of individuals, and in this contract, the effects of other contracts such as fetal deposit, gift interest (in the case of altruistic surrogate uterus contract) Renting a surrogate mother There is also a commercial type of breastfeeding contract, a sale with donation of sperm, eggs and embryos, which makes it difficult to attach this contract to a rented person. Also, the effects and exclusive terms of this contract can not be compared with the lease of individuals. In addition, these problems are more pronounced in cases where sperm, eggs or other embryos are used in the alternative uterine method. As some jurists have explicitly pointed out, "It does not seem unreasonable to place an agreement governing the use of an alternative uterus under the traditional title of rent (or rent of persons) in all cases." In the case where the egg is the surrogate mother, the contract is not just a lease of the uterus or a person, but a combination of a contract for the use of the egg and her uterus. (Jafarzadeh, 1991, p. 83)

Therefore, the uterine contract is an alternative to a combination of several contracts that have found an independent meaning and character in custom, and this contract can no longer be considered as one of its constituent contracts, but is an independent contract and is part of indefinite contracts.

3-6-3 Alternative uterus contract and labor contract:

In an alternative uterine contract in which infertile couples benefit from the services of a uterine woman, can the relationship between them be considered an employment contract? Is this contract subject to labor law? The important point in this case is that the belief in the rule of labor law over a surrogate contract is a sub-belief that the surrogate contract is inherently a lease contract because: An employment contract is a type of lease that is outside the scope of civil law. And is subject to certain regulations. Since the employment contract is subject to a special legal system and equal to it, one party (worker) enjoys protections and the other party is obliged to observe these rights and protections, distinguish the employment contract from other rental contracts and the uterine contract Alternatives are important.

Article 1 of a labor law defines a worker: "According to this law, a worker is a person who works in any capacity on behalf of the employer in return for a salary or wages."

From the term "employer" it can be understood that the worker's obedience and legal citizenship of the employer is the main basis of the employment contract.

Therefore, it can be said that in all cases where the hired person obeys the tenant's order in carrying out the work he is responsible for or is economically subordinate and the profit and loss of his work reaches him, their relations are governed by the labor law and in The cases in which the hired person works for himself and how to fulfill the obligation is with him and in this respect is not under the command and supervision of the tenant, the civil law applies. (Katozian, 1993, vol. 1, p. 564)

It is clear from this that the surrogacy contract cannot be considered a kind of labor contract and subject to labor law, because in this contract, the surrogate mother does not work under the command and supervision of the parents, and how to fulfill the obligation is up to her.

3-6-4 Alternative uterus contract and commodatum:

According to Article 607 of the Civil Code, a deposit is a contract under which a person transfers his property to another in order to keep it for free. What constitutes the substance and requirement of a deposit is the transfer of money for the purpose of "maintenance" to another, and must be returned to its owner upon the first claim. (Katozian, 2008, vol. 2, p. 4)

The main obligation in a pregnancy surrogacy contract can also be an obligation to maintain a fertilized egg or embryo, without being paid or received in exchange; This means that the parents or the applicant, according to the agreement, transfer the fertilized egg or the fetus to the surrogate mother without paying a bitch, so that she can take care of it, and the surrogate mother can take care of the fertilized egg without receiving a bitch, or The fetus is committed for a certain period of time.

Of course, the contract of succession will not be a mere deposit and maintenance, and the fulfillment of the main obligation by the surrogate mother will require other sub-tasks such as fertility using assisted reproductive methods, upbringing and childbirth.

So there may be doubts about whether the contract is a surrogate deposit or a rental. In order to remove such doubts and better distinguish the nature of the contract of succession in pregnancy, it is necessary to refer to the main goal and the basic commitment that arises as a result of the agreement between the parents and the surrogate mother, and separate it from the intentions and secondary obligations.

In the case where the main purpose is to maintain a fertilized egg or embryo, the contract should be considered a deposit; However, the trustee performs another service or services, and in the case of a contract for the purpose of performing a service or the acquisition of a special benefit by the surrogate mother in exchange for a certain exchange, the rules of rent of persons shall prevail; However, the maintenance of a fertilized egg or embryo is also necessary as a prerequisite for fulfilling the main obligation (Kanouzian, 1995, p. 25)

Despite the above, it seems that the main purpose of the succession contract in pregnancy is to maintain the fertilized egg or the fetus by the surrogate mother, and it is very difficult to imagine such a claim; Because normally in the uterine contract, there is no substitute for keeping the sperm as the main direction of the contract desired by the parties.

The act of placing the fetus in the womb is for the purpose of nurturing it, not for maintenance, and the surrogate mother accepts it for nurturing in her womb, not for maintenance, which she returns whenever the real parents demand it. However, the main obligation (fetal development in the womb) requires maintenance, which in this contract is maintenance as a sub-obligation in order to fulfill the main obligation. Therefore, the replacement uterus contract cannot be consistent with the structure of the deposit contract.

Therefore, if it turns out that the main purpose of the parties is not the maintenance of property, their relationship is not subject to the rules of the deposit agreement.

3-6-5 Alternative uterus contract and loan contract:

According to Article 635 of the Civil Code: "A loan is a contract by which one of the parties allows the other party to benefit from his property free of charge." Although the loan is given to the borrower for profit, what is actually the subject of the loan is the benefit. (Ibid., P. 14)

Now, if we consider the surrogate mother's contract as borrowed, then the surrogate mother allows the parents to benefit from one of their organs, which is the normal functioning of the woman's uterus. In this way, the surrogate mother creates the right to use one of her body parts for the parents, a ruling regarding the desired benefit, which, considering that the human right to her limbs and organs is a personal right, the surrogate mother does not have the right to Even create for others in your body parts and organs. (Nayebzadeh, 2001, p. 157)

In addition, the surrender of the loaned property and its receipt by the beneficiary and the possibility of returning it to the recipient (surrogate mother) is not possible in the replacement uterus contract. Thus, the replacement uterus contract is not applicable to the loan contract.

3-6-6 Alternative uterus contract and contract of reward:

According to Article 561 of the Civil Code: "Forgery is the obligation of a person to pay a certain reward for an action, whether the party is definite or indefinite."

Some legal writers believe that the nature of the surrogacy contract is compatible with the forgery contract (Moeini, 2008, p. 29). Some people believe that a replacement uterine contract is permissible before and after pregnancy to correct the recent problems. (Rahimi, 1989, p. 24).

Others suggested that in order to find a solution to these problems, the fake contract should be concluded in addition to the necessary contract. (Alizadeh, Anonymous, p. 159)

However, according to the above, although it is possible to apply the changes of the surrogate contract in accordance with the forgery contract by applying some changes, but in the current situation, considering the real characteristics of these two contracts in the Iranian legal system, the surrogate uterus can be adapted to the forgery contract. Does not have.

3-6-7 Alternative uterus contract and Contract of settlement:

A peace is an agreement to create or repeal one or more legal effects without subject to the specific provisions of certain contracts. (Jafari Langroudi, 1989, p. 157). Also, in any case where the existence of a right between two persons is doubtful, or has been disputed, or the purpose is to avoid a possible conflict, a contract based on this and mutual forgiveness of the parties is peace. (Katozian, 2006, vol. 1, p. 280).

Some, considering the acceptance of the broad concept of peace in the Civil Code and Articles 758, 754 and 752 of this law; It is believed that the agreement of the infertile couple to use the surrogate mother's womb to transport their fetus and finally the delivery of the baby to the infertile couple is realized in the form of a peace contract, so that on the one hand the written will of the couple Infertile and on the other hand is the will of the surrogate mother, which leads to the emergence of legal action in the form of a peace contract. (Dehghani, 2008, p. 159).

Although this view may seem correct, it should be noted that the nature of the surrogacy contract is not compatible with a peace agreement. As we know, individuals not only in the alternative uterus contract but also in all other specific contracts such as sale, etc. can conclude them in the form of a peace contract and achieve their goal of concluding the contract without the effects of that specific format being enforceable by the legislator. Have. But it must be the goal of the parties to the peace agreement or it must be specified in the contract. Therefore, although the parties can conclude an alternative uterus contract in the form of a peace contract, regardless of any format we consider for it, but the mere nature of the replacement uterus contract is not compatible with a peace contract.

3-6-8 Alternative uterus contract and adoption contract:

A group of Sunni jurists believe that the uterine contract replaces the nature of the adoption contract because the ultimate goal of this contract is to attribute the lineage of the child born to it to the ruling mother, or in other words, the lineage from the surrogate mother to the egg-holding mother or ruling mother. It should be conveyed that this is the same as adoption (Morsi, 1993, p. 180).

This group of jurists has ruled that this agreement is invalid because there is no adoption in Islam. As the laws of some Islamic countries explicitly prohibit adoption (Algerian Family Law, Article 96 and Kuwait Law on Personal Status, Article 167).

In the case law of Iran, adoption is not recognized as having legal effects related to lineage, and only in the case of protection of orphaned children, adoption has legal effects.

This theory is considered because according to the laws of some countries (French Civil Code, Article 334), adoption is correct and has legal effects. As a result, this contract can be considered as a prenatal adoption contract. But it seems that the surrogate contract cannot be considered the nature of the adoption contract; Because this theory is based on the fact that in the surrogate mother we consider the surrogate mother as the real mother of the child (Mehrpour, 2003, p. 160). While according to most Shiite jurists, the owner of the egg is the real mother of the child, as a result, according to Shiite jurists, there is no substitute for the transfer of lineage due to the uterine contract, so that we consider this contract as adoption.

Some Shiite jurists have explicitly stated that the use of a surrogate uterus has nothing to do with adoption, and that a child born in this way is only a relative of the surrogate mother, but in terms of lineage rules belongs to the owners of the sperm.   Makarem Shirazi, 2016, Istifta'at section; Rezania Moallem, 2004, p. 463; Ayatollah Yazdi, 2015, p. 465)

3-6-9 Alternative uterine contract and private agreement:

In view of the above, it seems that the mother contract is a substitute for an independent contract with its own requirements and effects. The main requirement of this contract is the commitment of the surrogate mother to carry the fetus for the benefit of the applicant couple and to deliver the child to them after delivery. Which may be done as compensation or non-compensation (altruistic. Considering the above, in Iranian law such agreements are anonymous contracts and can be analyzed in the context of the verse "Amnesty with contracts" and Article 10 of the Civil Code. (Nayebzadeh, 2001, p. 159; Jalalian, 2007, p. 329; Rakhshandeh, p. 384).

According to Article 10 of the Civil Code: "Private contracts are valid for those who have concluded them, unless it is explicitly against the law."

This theory also has many supporters among the jurists of the Arab countries. These jurists have stated that the surrogacy contract is different from all the specific contracts mentioned by the law and has similarities with only some of them. As a result, this contract is inherently an indefinite contract. And has its unique and special nature according to the purpose of the parties to this contract (Mehran, 2002, p. 613)

Another reason for this claim is that by analyzing the surrogate contract, we come to the conclusion that the sum of the different obligations contained in this contract cannot be attributed to a single contract, because this contract, A contract consists of several definite and indefinite contracts, if this contract can be used for fetal deposit contracts, interest (in the case of a altruistic surrogate uterus contract), surrogate mother rent (commercial type), a contract for breastfeeding, sale or donation of sperm, The egg and embryo decomposed. In determining the nature of this type of composite contracts and determining the rules that govern such contracts, it is better to analyze the common intention and the basis of compromise between the parties to the contract.

Conclusion:

The following results are obtained from all the aforementioned materials in the present article.

- The surrogate uterus contract is one of the new methods of infertility treatment, according to which a woman who is called a surrogate mother agrees to use assisted reproductive methods to produce the fetus from sperm and ovum of an infertile couple and to apply for a uterus so this couple called Judgment parents or third parties carry the sperm that was found in the artificial insemination laboratory environment into their womb, and after the baby is born, it delivers it to the parents, who may receive a fee from the surrogate mother to perform the procedure, It is called an exchange contract or to do so solely for humanitarian reasons based on kinship or friendship, which is called an irrevocable contract.

- There are different situations related to the subject of embryo implanted in the uterus of a rented woman. Some jurists believe that this woman and her child born from her womb do not have special rules because it has no such relationship with the owner of the uterus genetically, except after birth that the owner of the uterus breastfeeds him and makes foster intimate according to Article 1046. Breastfeeding kinship is relative kinship in terms of the sanctity of marriage. Foster relationship is like affinity relationship in terms of the sanctity of marriage.

- Pregnancy in the method of alternative uterus, in which the fetus was from the ovum of a foreign woman or a surrogate mother, the opinion of most jurists is that such a method is not allowed. Because the formation of the sperm and consequently the fetus must be by inoculation of the ovum and sperm of a man and a woman, between which there is a marital relationship, whether permanent or temporary. Also, in determining the lineage of such infants, the jurists consider the infant to be attributed to the legal parents of the owners of ovum and sperm, and consider the surrogate mother as a priority, the breastfeeding mother of the child, with whom only marriage is forbidden, but other traces such as inheritance or custody will not be included.

References:

The Holy Quran

A: Persian Sources

Books:

1- Akhundi and Behjati Ardakani, Mohammad and Zohreh, Alternative womb, Tehran, Study Organization and

Compilation of humanities books of universities (Samat), second edition, 2008

2- Ebrahimi Fakhar, Hamidreza and Kouhestani, Hamidreza and Baghchaghi, Nayreh, level reduction

Hoshyari, first edition, Hayan, Tehran, 2002

3- Emami and Safaei, Assadollah and Seyed Hossein, Family Law, Tehran, Mizan Publishing, 2010

4- Jafari Langroudi, Mohammad Jafar, Family Law, Tehran, Ganj-e-Danesh, 2006

5- Mohammad Jafar, Extensive Legal Terminology, Treasure of Knowledge, 2008

6- Hamdollahi, Asif Roshan, Mohammad, Comparative jurisprudential and legal study of the contract of use Alternative uterus, first edition, Tehran, Majd Publications, 2009

7- Dehghani, Hossein, Alternative womb, Law of the Day, No. 5, 2008,

8- Rezania Moallem, Mohammad Reza, Medical Fertility from the Perspective of Jurisprudence and Law, First Edition, Book Garden Publications, Qom, 2004

9- Rahimi, Habibollah, civil liability arising from surrogacy, fertility and infertility, 1387, No. 2

10- Shahidi, Mehdi, Collection of Legal Articles, First Edition, Tehran, Lawyer Publishing, 2006

11- Safaei, Seyed Hossein, Non-Contractual Requirements, Tehran Mizan, 2010

12- Comparative study of family law, Tehran, 2008 , Specialized Journal of Theology, »The nature of the contract , Resources 117

14. Divine grace, salvation, embryo donation and other assisted reproduction methods in Iranian law, Tehran, Jangal Publications, 2010

15. Civil Law of the Islamic Republic of Iran, Collection of Legal Laws and Regulations, Compilation, Jahangir Man Soor, Tehran, Doran Publications, 2012

16- Law on how to donate embryos to infertile couples, approved in 2003, set of rules and regulations, Family, edited by Seyed Mehdi Kamalan, Tehran, Kamalan Publications, third edition, 2010

17- Katozian, Nasser, Requirements outside the contract, Tehran, Mizan Publishing, 2010

18- Family Law, Third Edition, Tehran, Mizan Publishing, 2014

19- Civil Law, Certain Contracts, Fourth Edition, Winter, Publishing Company, In collaboration with Bahman Borna Company, 2008

20- General Rules of Contracts, 5 volumes, publishing company in cooperation with the company, Bahman Borna, second edition, 1390

21- Mohaghegh Damad, Seyed Mostafa, Jurisprudential and legal study of the marriage family and its dissolution, Tehran, Islamic Sciences Publishing Center, 2010

22- Rules of Jurisprudence, Civil Section, Volume 2, Samat Publications, 1995, 2008, The Voice of Justice, No. 37 "A word about an alternative womb"

24- Nayebzadeh, Abbas, Legal Review of New Methods of Artificial Reproduction, Tehran, Majd, 2001

Articles:

1- Akhoondi, Mohammad Mehdi, Familiarity with in vitro fertilization and the necessity of using gametes 118 References Alternatives in the treatment of infertility, collection of articles on gamete and embryo donation, second issue, 2005

2- Behjati Ardakani, Zohreh, Assessment and Health Consultation and Donor Conformity, Journal, Infertility Research, No. 8, 2001

3- Rezania Moallem, Mohammad Reza, Medical Fertility from the Perspective of Jurisprudence and Law, Jurisprudence Research Institute, And Islamic Law, 2007

4. Rouhani, Mohammad Sadegh, paper presented at the symposium on the jurisprudential and legal status of transfer, Jenin, 2016

5. Sadeghi Moghadam, Mohammad Hassan, jurisprudential principles and requirements of the law on how to donate embryos to Infertile couples, 2016 p. 46

6- Safaei, Seyed Hossein, Article on the inadequacies of Iranian law on gamete and embryo donation with Attention to comparative law, two quarterly journals of jurisprudence and family law (Nedaye Sadegh), Imam University 2001, Sadegh, No. 4

7- Mehrpour, Hossein, An Attitude Towards the Legal and Religious Status of Artificial Reproduction, Research Journal 1997, Law, Faculty of Law, Shahid Beheshti University, No. 19

-8 "Analysis of jurisprudential rules of lineage in a child born from a surrogate womb", Naseri Moghadam, Hossein, Reproduction and Infertility Quarterly, Tehran, 2008

Theses:

1. Salehi, Zeinab, Thesis of rented uterus and gamete donation, Kashan Azad University, 2006

-2 Solati, Fatemeh, Thesis on the jurisprudential principles of gamete donation, Payame Noor University Markazi, 2009 Resources 119

B: Arabic Sources:

1: Qomi, Mirza Abolghasem, Jame Al-Shattat, University of Tehran Press

2- Isfahani, Mohammad Hossein Company, margin of the book Al-Makasib for Isfahan, I, Hadith, 5 volumes, Anwar al-Huda, Qom, Iran, first, 1423

3- Khomeini, Ruhollah, Al-Bayy, 5 volumes, third edition, Al-Adab Press, 1427

4- Tahrir al-Wasila, 2 volumes, Institute Dar Al-Alam Press, 1409

5- Khoei, Seyyed Abolghasem, Basics of completing the curriculum, Najaf, Al-Adab Press, Bita

6- Minhaj Al-Saleheen, Qom, General City of Ayatollah Khoei, 1414

7- Ragheb Esfahani, Hussein, Vocabulary in Gharib Al-Quran, Qom Book Publishing Office, Bita

8- Tabatabai, Seyyed Mohammad Hussein, Al-Mizan Fi Tafsir Al-Quran, Qom Farhang Publications, Islamic, 1995

9- Tabarsi, Fadl Ibn Hassan, Jame 'Al-Jame', correction and suspension - Abolghasem Gorji -Tehran University of Tehran Press, Bita

10- Ameli, Mohammad Ibn Maki (the first martyr), Rules and Benefits, Qom, Jamiat Publications Teachers, 1400

11- Ameli, Free, Shiite means to study Sharia issues, Tehran, Islamia, Bita

12- Makarem Shirazi, Nasser, Rules of Jurisprudence, School of Imam Amir Al-Momenin 2007

13- Maki Ameli, Zainuddin, Al-Rawdha Al-Bahiya, Qom, Islamic Enlightenment Institute, 2006

14- Mousavi Bojnourdi, Seyed Mohammad Hassan, Jurisprudential Rules, 2 volumes, Orouj Institute, 2010

www.ingramcontent.com/pod-product-compliance
Lightning Source LLC
Chambersburg PA
CBHW032116280326
41933CB00009B/865